LOOSE CHANGE
the Pieces
up
Picking

Poetry & Prose by
S.Z. PUTNAM

2022

Copyright © 2022 Read or Green Books
Albuquerque, New Mexico

Cover Art by Shane Manier, Guerilla Poets, founder

All rights reserved. No portion of this publication may be reproduced or transmitted in any form without prior permission of **S.Z. Putnam** unless such copying is expressly permitted by Federal copyright law. Addresses, questions, comments send to: Read or Green Books: marissa@ReadorGreenBooks.com.

Visit our websites:
www.ReadorGreenBooks.com
www.ShaneManier.com
www.SZPutnamPens.com

FIRST EDITION
ISBN: 978-1-7378163-4-8
Produced in the United States of America

To Alice, Elliot, and Izabel:
May your light always shine bright
to guide you through the darkness.
For you are the light
guiding me
when this universe dims.

To Gabe:
May you continue to find courage
in fighting for yourself and in fighting for love.
At your very core, your heart is the essence of beauty.
My hope is for you to find joy again
in the precious moments of life.

LOOSE CHANGE

the Pieces
up
Picking

Resources for Help Regarding Substance Abuse:

Substance Abuse & Mental Health Services Administration (SAMHSA):
1-800-662-HELP (4357)
https://www.samhsa.gov/find-help/national-helpline

Al-Anon: for family and friends.
https://al-anon.org

AA: Alcoholics Anonymous
https://aa.org

CONTENTS

LOVE & ABANDONED WISHES 1
   THE FIRST TIME 2
   IN LOVE 4
   NOTHING 5
   DO YOU REMEMBER LIGHTNING? 6
   TATTOOED 8
   INACCESSIBLE LOVE 9
   MUSINGS ON THE SUN 10
   FALLING STARS 11
   CONNECTION 12
   LAZY IN LOVE 13
   YOU ARE… 14

CHANGE 15
   LOOSE CHANGE 16
   INSIGNIFICANT 18
   DROWNING 19
   RUNAWAY 20
   2 A.M. THOUGHTS 23
   FIRE FLIES 24
   THE WAITING GAME 25
   INK 26
   COUNTING CHANGE 28
   HE LIES TO ME 30

HOPE FLOATS 32
WHAT'S THE "MATTER" WITH LOVE?................... 33
BATTLEFIELD 34
I LOST YOU 35
MY MASTERPIECE 36
LADY OF THE LAKE 38

PIGGY'S FULL...**40**

THE MISTRESS 41
THE STONE COLLECTOR... 44
DISORIENTATION 46
THE SIEGE... 48
LOVE IS BLIND 50
JUST IN CASE 52
MILLIONAIRE.. 54
SUBSTANCE 56
WHOLE 57
CABIN ON THE POND 58
HOPE CHEST.. 59

CRACK… **60**

HOME 61
BLINDSIDED 62
WATERBOARDING 64
HOMICIDE 66
REPLICATE 67

CODEPENDENCY 68
SAND CEREMONY 70
SNOW 71
THE OPPONENT 72
HOUSE OF CARDS 73
THE BOMB 74
EXTINCTION 75

...SHATTER 76

THE GREAT ESCAPE 77
WHEN WRITE IS LEFT BEHIND 78
READY OR NOT 80
WOULD YOU KNOW IT? 81
HOSTAGE 82
BRAVE 83
FATHER FIGURE 84
BABY SOPRANO 85
INNER TURMOIL 86
DEAR GOD 88
LETTERS TO THE WIND 89
FROZEN RIVER 90
I'LL LOVE YOU LIKE A SHADOW 92
DISTASTEFUL SONG 93
WHAT ARE YOU GOING TO DO? 94
SHADES OF TRAUMA 95

LOOK 96
HOW DO WE REWIND TIME? 97

PICKING UP THE PIECES 98

FAULT LINE 99
SILENCE 100
CANDLES 101
WANTING AND NEEDING 102
THE LIGHTHOUSE (KUV TXIV) 104
THE WARRIOR (KUV NIAM) 105
INSIDIOUS 106
HOW DO I LOVE YOU? 107
NOURISHMENT 108
COMPOSING 109
BEACONS 110
A DECIPHERED PROMISE 111
INSIDE YOUR SKIN 112
THE FOREST 113
THE HUNTER 114
LITTLE BOY 115
FLUIDITY 116
MEAT IN THE MIDDLE 117
THE MASK 118
RESCUED WISHES 120
WORTHY 122

Introduction

My poetry collection is a look into the harsh reality of addiction and the emotional damage that occurred when addiction took over my life. I was overcoming grief from three failed pregnancies when I was then faced with my failing marriage. I could not figure out the loss of our connection as a couple until addiction revealed itself to me, in the form of the man I love.

I started on a journey of self-healing because I was lost, and I no longer loved myself as I once did. It was through the action of my first faltering steps that I could start healing. This journey allowed me to finally recognize just how far addiction was willing to go to destroy everything I love, including all the lives revolving around its vicious cycle.

My pieces are utterly raw and painful at times, mimicking the cycle of substance abuse and my own emotional response to it. And though this is a difficult topic to discuss and express, my pieces are about love and the effects of love.

These words are my thoughts, pouring out, in my quest to rediscover connection, hope, healing, and love. My hope is for anyone reading my journey, to know they are not alone. It is only together and through the sharing of our stories that we can help pull each other out of darkness, whatever it may be. And while I could be seen as a victim in this situation, it is not a role I am ready to accept.

LOVE & ABANDONED WISHES

THE FIRST TIME

I remember the first time
    I desired
        to be yours.
Clear blue sky
        dialed down
to blackened night.

Diamonds carefully strewn overhead
      as if
          by your design.
Fate was on your side.

A symphony
    played by
        Summer's caress
and crickets
      was our song.
Our melodic breathing
        the unintentional
           duet.

The flesh of my arms
    my neck
        my face
flushed scarlet.
Goosebumps arising
  to greet a firm and gentle touch.
Your hands
    held mine
with unfaltering strength
      while ironclad arms
    housed me
      in their haven.

The language of your body
        burned
  a hole in
      my defenses.
Charcoal eyes
    blazed
      with an
      uncontrollable
        fever.

Unspoken words
          promising me
     forever.

It was a single night
  of anticipation
      and longing
    for our souls to speak
          in harmony.

  You and I
      welcoming
    the sound.

IN LOVE

You should see her eyes.
They are glowing.
She is glowing.
She is in love.
There is no question about it.
There is no logic to it.
She has met the love of her life.
Her energy of certainty is as pliable as clay
       as physical as it is material.
She
    is in
  love.

NOTHING

I love him.
    I love him beyond anything I ever believed
        I would get in this life.
    He has me acting like a fool to stand up for an "Us"
        and I am willing to do it all
            sacrifice it all
          in the name of Love.

I love him.
    His love is like electricity.
        The shock of it jump-started my heart
    in ways I never knew I could feel.
And maybe you believe he brought me to life
    but he had me falling

        falling

        falling

        head-first into love
                instead.

I love him.
    For me
        there is no doubt
there is nothing in life that can go wrong
    as long as I have him by my side
        and as long as he has me.

        Nothing…

DO YOU REMEMBER LIGHTNING?

It was a lifetime ago.
      Almost forgotten
   this *memory* that allude*s* me
unless I search for it
        in the suitcases of my mind.

I packed them up
        stuffed full and put away
   for safekeeping.

Safekeeping…
     though I've forgotten where *"safe"* is.
        It happens all the time.
     Me
       losing things
  in the shadows of my sight.

This memory of *lightning*
   in Wisconsin-wet
      in
        Wisconsin-*unpredictable* weather.
.
It was a firestorm of litany
    both sides
       unwilling to agree.
     I was alone
  in a room designed for sleep
     though rest was not to be had.

And you…you took off
        and the doubts
     crept
         in.

When you returned
        you were *changed*.
   The *honesty* we shared that night
      is what dreams are made of.

You spoke of uncertainty
         and prayers to a god
    you no longer believed in.
   You described being surrounded
            by an *electric storm*
     flooding the entire sky
        except
where you stood.

You said
    it took your breath away.
        You told me
            you believed in that moment
      we were meant to be.

I *fell* in love with you then.
    Fell in love with the man
        you *wanted* to be
    the man
   you were *becoming*.
  The man
    who loved me
        through any
      through *all*
         adversity.

And I fell.

TATTOOED

You tattooed your love across my chest
Inked and colored at my behest.
An original piece pulled from the air.
It weaved around my heart with care.

The years passed on and the image faded.
The colors now lifeless and much degraded.
I am the *Canvas*, angry with my thoughts
of no longer caring for the *Artist's* loss.

So I *blackened* my chest to hide your art
but I couldn't quite cover the parts
that peeked and cried out to be seen
they bled right through as an *ugly seam*.

What a silly girl was I
to try and cover a love that died.
All the while *it remained*
tattooed on my heart and brain.

INACCESSIBLE LOVE

I am in love with inaccessible love
    and yet I can't stop myself.
  It's infuriating.
        It's like loving the Sun
            with myself as the Earth.

I feel the warmth and know it's there
      but I will never touch it.
      And someday
   the fires of its warmth
          may consume me
        destroying all that inhabits me…

And I just lay in wait
        for scorching warmth.

MUSINGS ON THE SUN

He was her *sunrise* and her *sunset*
   rousing her from slumber to seek the day
    soothing her to sleep.

                And she was fixated on the sky
          as a falling star faded into non-existence
                    wondering *when* and *if*
  her Sun would follow suit.

And she questioned whether to turn towards
    the luminescent Moon to soothe her
if the Sun disappeared
      for she would *always* turn towards the sky.

                    But
      would the Moon shine on *without* the Sun
              she wondered?
                The truth is, she may *never* know.

FALLING STARS

I used to love you as if you were the sun
        and I
                a twin soul from another galaxy.
    We burned for each other and became red giants
in our all-consuming passion.
           Our desires matched
                      in a raging inferno.

Burning
                burning
           burning…

                    Burning up.

We have been aging for eons now it seems
                our fires abating.
      No longer twin souls but nemesis
              engulfing all
                    as our fires brace to perish.

Perhaps it is better to dream
          we become the fallen stars
      that others wish upon
        hoping
   for a fevered love
     like
        ours
      once
            was.

CONNECTION

I curl into the expanse of your back
        trying to absorb the heat radiating from you
    to evaporate the desolation inside.
My single cheek is all I can meet
      and I am greeted with warmth
          from this single connection.
      It helps me melt for a moment.
  And I sigh quietly
          as I watch the slightest onset
      of steam
            rise
      and
    float
      away.

LAZY IN LOVE

We had it…we had what we lost
    for a mere minute.
      Sitting there selling ourselves to
        "Yeah! We're in it!"
But honestly, Babe
    we are borderline crazy
      'cause the love that we have
        is nothing but lazy.

Moments shared are not so precious
    our laughter and kisses no longer infectious.
      And still
    we love the dream of being loved
but we live a fool's errand in loving to judge.

We continue to sit here wasting our time
    yelling and blaming the other
      for all of their crimes.
We wish and wish and wish and wish
    but nothing goes our way.
      Just sitting here hoping we're enough
      to last another day.

The effort it takes…on paper
    seems so simple
    but then throw in our tempers
      and our love becomes fickle.
We're just two stubborn people
    too in and out of love.
      'cause again
    we are too lazy
    in our devotion to our love.

YOU ARE…

You are my greatest love

                       and

                                         my greatest deception…

CHANGE

LOOSE CHANGE

Penny for a thought of yours.
    Thoughts…
  I would pay so much more than that.
      And I have paid
    in the currency exchange of my heart.

Each tear I've dropped
      the loose change remaining
          from my *unspent* words
    kept in my piggy bank.

Piggy's full.
    Brimming full.
  Full to the point of *explosion*
        with no more space to *breathe*
no more room to encourage the wondrous
      clinking joy, from the collection within.

I come upon a wishing well
     abandoned and dried up
   from long ago
along with the *wishes* that were made in it.
       All that remains are the pennies
    conducting the chilled stones.
  Pennies…
      change,
    that no one wants
        but me…

I try hurriedly to collect them all
     clumsy in my haste.
       Try…
So, so, so many wishes.
    Wondering if I can collect them all?

I'm on my knees, chest full of questions
        gathering the change
           collecting
                myself.

Energy *spent* on the wrong task
        more change unspent.
    I leave the change in the wishing well
            there's too much to collect.
        I'll come back another day
            with another piggy.

Defeated by my failed task
    I go home to alleviate this weight I now bear.
        But I couldn't.
    I can't…

I'm *full* now
        much like my piggy
too full of change unspent.
            You try and add a penny.
    It doesn't fit.
            You're frustrated.
                As am I…

You poke a little harder and I   *C R A   C K…*
    …S H A T T E R.
                Each piece hurls out
from the destruction of this home for loose change.
        Hurls at you.

I lose myself in an endless scream
                bottom of the wishing well.
    Loose change spent.
        But not on a *wish*.
        Not on a *dream*…

INSIGNIFICANT

I am insignificant
    especially to you.
  When I am gone
and my spoken words evaporate
    when words penned have faded
  who will remember me?

And it comes in torrent waves
    these doubts
  that come crashing in.
At its very peak
    I am unlovable
  to the one
      I love.

DROWNING

I saw your tears slam down to the earth
    like rain.
  Your beautiful smile disappeared
      behind the clouds of your palms
    as you concealed your hurt
        from the raging storms.

Heartache was written like a book
      across your face.
  You soaked the ground
     but the storm did not dissipate.
And I wondered
    if you would drown yourself
      with your sorrows.

RUNAWAY

Did you know
      that I ran away?
  The house was cold and empty
          on that particular day.

I was cold.

All the blankets
  broken-in
      upon our bed in a heap
  could not warm me.
          Could not warm the empty bed.

I was empty.

The absence of you
    a part of my void
        and I could not fill it.
          Not in this moment
        hard as I tried.

So, I ran away.

  Did you notice?
      Did you even
    realize?

I didn't pack a single thing
   just grabbed my phone and wallet.
      I needed my phone
  in case you noticed
       noticed I was gone.
I needed you to want me
    enough for you to call.

I took my wallet
    'cause I didn't know
  didn't know
      where I was going.
     Phone and wallet and keys…
I jump in my car and I go.
     Still no destination in mind.
      And then
    here I am…

"Am" is the parking lot
     of the local hospital.
    I don't know why I came here.
Only thing that I can think of is
  hospitals are where people go
    for help.

And I needed help.
    My heart was dying.

I parked and I stayed
    but I didn't go in
   'cause I was bleeding on the inside
     and I knew
   no one could see that pain.

I spent the night.
    I was chilled to the bones
  but at least
    I could feel.
And when the morning light
     brushed upon my face
    I wiped my tear-stained
  sleep-filled eyes
    and I was on my way…

...to my empty house
        to my empty bed
    to my worn-out blankets
              with my worn-down head.

And to this day
        you never knew
    I was a runaway.

    'cause
you never called to look for me
    you never made it home
           and when you saw my face that night
    I hid my broken heart
from your sightless eyes.

I still drive by hospitals...

        I still can't forget.

2 A.M. THOUGHTS

Sitting in the car with my bare feet curled up close against my body. I'm in the driveway looking at my home. In the driver's seat with nowhere to go. It's cold out. The chilly sort of summer cold that seeps into my bones.

But while my body is shivering, I am numb to the cold because an angst has taken over me.

I don't know why.

All I know is I'm contemplating what the future holds and questioning what I want.

My heart wants an unreachable future.
My body remains in the present.
My brain is trapped in the past.

And I don't know why I feel this way…

FIRE FLIES

Fireflies in the darkened night
        light up the trees
                    amongst
          tar-stained
               woods.
      I was lonely where I stood.

Fire flies up
      off a crackling log
    escaping
           and
reaching
      for oxygen.
               "Feed me"
the dancing flame says
              gulping more air.

In *desperation* from starvation
      it reaches too high and
          "poof"
a piece of it disappears
    like
        it never
            was…

But it keeps on dancing anyway
                    Like *ME*.
        To a tune only
           it
        can
            hear…

THE WAITING GAME

We were both dying inside
               next to each other
     miles apart emotionally
needing the other's love as much as air
          and waiting for the other person to see it…

INK

Ink smeared on my hand today.
    I knew not where it came from
though I had calculated suspicion as to the culprit
    like much of the distressing events in my life.

My mind
    straining from lack of knowledge
reaching towards answers in a black hole.
    I feel deflated.

The ink started as a few blots before spreading.
    Spreading as I tried
        unsuccessfully
      to remove it from my hands.

It began seeping into my pores
    and I am absorbing
  retaining
      all its darkness.

It is suffocating.

The longer I worked to remove it
    the larger the spread and the larger the stain.
The larger the stain
      the harder I scrubbed.
    Skin raw from my futile efforts.

I could not get it off
      just like I could not forget my pain.
    My pain was harrowing
      like this ink on my hand
        …hands now.

It is everywhere
  clouding the bits of me I did not know existed
 staining the curved lines of my fingerprints
   getting
  as deep as the grooves.

I cannot rid myself of it
   hard as I try
and after a while
  I just want to forget it is there
   but
 it is noticeable
    to me.

So I put myself to task
  washing with water
as hot as my
   scalding
    tears.

And though Grandfather Time and effort
  helped to clean and wipe away the stain
 there are remnants of this event in my pores
  of this moment

   of

 this
  pain.

COUNTING CHANGE

Why are you fighting to keep us in the past?
      I know what you want is for our love to last.
    But when we take two steps forward
          and five steps back
        I worry so much
           about how the *coins* stack.

And you want so much
    to get through this and mend
        but all I see
      is you're not keeping your end.

   Is there a reason
      that I cannot see?
'cause your words are going
          on a *spending* spree.

They fill me
     and fill me
   and fill me to the brim
but you are not *feeding* devotion
           you are *stealing* my grin.

    And I just do not know
       what we are fighting for.
I hope the answer is love.
      I am hoping for more.

And the stacks of change
    they are growing higher
 and higher.
    I just hope we're not counting
        on when love will retire.

So I reach on over
      to knock a stack down.
It crashes to the floor
          making much needed sound.

I get up and walk away
      'cause no matter what I say
   you are no longer one
          whom I can persuade…

and I know…I

        I

   cannot

        make
    you

    stay.

HE LIES TO ME

He lies to me
        and he
    doesn't think I can tell.

It's in the way he looks at me
      and he doesn't see me.
    It's in the way he speaks to me
      but he doesn't converse.
         It's in the way he touches me
    without connection.

I know he is lying.
      He just doesn't know
    I know.

He lies to me
  and all I can think of
      is how scared he must be
  keeping his fears to himself.
Keeping the doubts crowded about.

He hides from me
    as if I have not encountered his demons.
  They chase me relentlessly
    in the light of day
        and also in my dreams.

He shields his Self
    from facing pain
  and he thinks it is not visible
    on the lines of his face
  they are screaming
      to be seen
          …it is torture for me.

It is so apparent
      to me
           his pain.
And yet
   there is nothing I can do
      for his self-imposed shame.

He lies to me
   and my chest knee-jerks in reaction.
It is an olive pit
         peach pit
     solid rock-pitted
        weight in my gut.

We are both alone
     banished to separate quarters of doubt
   by his choosing
and I cannot break the walls
   that lean in to suffocate me.

I cannot gut the leaded chains
     connecting stomach and heart
   though it is what I need.
           …WE need.

Alone.
     Lonely.
               Suffering.
        Pain.

He lies to me
   and I wonder
     of my remaining days
   will this pain be all my mind retains?

HOPE FLOATS

You *inhale*
        and take a drag
     pulling the wisps of smoke
               into your lungs
            like the poison of expectations.

                  You *exhale*
          keeping the cancer inside you
             smothering the remnants of life still present.
    Hope is bonded with the smoke
and is just as weightless.
                You release it.
                     It floats
                  away.

              Fingers grasping for tendrils of vapors.
          You cannot hold or acquire the intangible.
So *you inhale*
to find some peace.
    How's
        that
            going?

            You exhale.

        Does
                Hope float?

          Or does it

                choke

                you?

WHAT'S THE "MATTER" WITH LOVE?

The words are there
          as if etched in on glass.
    Beautiful in its promise.
                Fragile in its design.

    Or maybe
        more like
the words are there
      like the buds on the tip of your tongue.
          I can almost taste it
        though I can't.

The "I love you..."
          The "I love you(s)..."
  They appear to vanish as quickly
        as their formulated sounds.

      If my heart were a balloon
perhaps I could siphon the air from your lungs
          to keep it afloat.
    The air is hot enough…

The air is hot
      and the words are
    forged
      in fire.

Can we temper our love like weapons?
    Wield our hearts so as not to shatter
      from the pressure?
  Or will we go up in the flames
        consumed like the "matter"
            keeping Love
      alive?

BATTLEFIELD

We   SLICED
open
                      W O U N D S
in each other's heart
with every cruel   ARSENAL
we carried.
Every
word
                      FIRED
escalating
static
                      TENSION
on the battlefield.
Increasing
in   FORCE
'til blackened air was so thick
even   BULLETS
could no longer penetrate
invisible   ARMOR.
It was in this fashion
we bulletproofed our hearts
'til we were more   STRANGERS
than friends
more   ENEMIES
than lovers.
And it was in this battle
we   LOST
ourselves
our trust
and
                                D E S T R O Y E D
one
another.

I LOST YOU

You withdrew from me so unexpectedly
    I didn't notice you were *missing*
      until you were *gone*.
  Like a mitten from last season
    the single sock
        the spare key
           the last puzzle piece…
   GONE.

So many moments I felt I almost lost you.
    So many…

Our shared lifetime of this?
      It takes my breath
   every time you *slip*.

If I were being honest
    I recall the night I *lost* you
        though it's a fading   *M E M O   R   Y.*

I was too scared to verbalize your demise.
      Sitting there
   your refracted stare of despair
        the one I had started to notice
    but never dared to compare.

I was *paralyzed* by it all.

You transformed into a fraction of yourself
    finding distraction.
   And eyes that I once begged to drown in
      were slowly drowning *me*.

I knew that night *I   L O S T   YOU.*

MY MASTERPIECE

My masterpiece is almost complete.
The swirls of anger and rage at life's despair
are strewn across this canvas in jagged lines
most likely from my agitated movements.

Wet acrylic stench mixed in with days of unrest
is wafting off into the air.
I'm high from the fumes
or maybe it's the sleep deprivation.

Either way
        I can't stop now.
Not when I'm so close to completion.

I'm enraged
        deranged
     demented.
I cannot morph this piece fast enough.

The image it covers is my novice-piece
an innocent portrayal of love.
Beautiful lines and shapes so smooth
you could cut them like butter.

Perfection.
        Or so I thought.

Heartbreak gilded in pieces so small
that they started as flecks on this piece
changing this work of art
changing me.

'til one day I took a step back and looked
        and I realized…this painting was different.

No longer was this love
this was unadulterated fury.
Fury at life
     the Fates
   the gods.

Anything and anyone.
For no one could explain my heart's ache
    choking me off
      like a fire without air.

I run my paint-stained fingers across the piece.
I trace every line.
I feel every tormenting groove.
This was destruction at my finest.

My masterpiece…

LADY OF THE LAKE

I walk down to the shore of this lake.
Wildflowers are growing everywhere
    spreading their fragrance around me
    drowning me in their soft but heady scent.

Peace is much needed
    when so many questions plague my mind like locusts.
    I am in a *cyclical* state of confusion I cannot escape
        and I am constantly questioning myself.

I sit down and look out at the mirrored lake.
Something pulls my gaze downwards.
    A force so strong
    it feels like strings attached to my sockets.

I cannot turn my gaze away.

Before me
    appearing like a siren from the sea
    a steadfast lady, comfortable in her element.
        In control of her breeze-like aura.
.
A warrior princess she appeared
        with wild tresses blowing all about.
    I am captivated by her striking energy
    her palpable forcefield.

She is magnetic.

Her knowing smile hints of her *resilience*
        and
    I am eager
        for her truths.

I bow my head down to the waters in prayer.
    Wishes pour out of me instead
                like a flood of currents.

I channel this beautiful being
        emulating her poise
                reflecting her serenity
    refracting
        my loneliness.

I feel a wave of words flowing across my lips
        like the breeze in the wind.
            Effortless.

Jolted awake from my trance
        as lips
                meet the cool water's caress.
    I stare into my reflection
a renewed promise of love in my chest.
                And in this moment, I have clarity.

I am *determined.*
                Renewed.
        Reborn.

I *will* get my answers
            and the tides engulfing me
        are finally
            going to *change*.

PIGGY'S FULL

THE MISTRESS

It started with simple un-truths
    barely mentionable in their miniscule size.
  Un-assuming un-truths
        so
     they were not mentioned
         to me…

The story begins
    you were once hers.
  You met her at a hangout
    as she knew friends from your *circle*
      and she was yours to be had
    if you wanted her.
        …and you did.

Not sure if you recall the beginning?
    Not sure I want to know.
  These armored secrets are locked up tight
    as you're keeping them
      out of sight.

Maybe
    you were star-crossed lovers
      like dear Romeo
          and Juliette
     kept apart by angry parents
  held hostage 'til the end.

How could they know
      the depth of your love
  of your infatuation?
  They forcibly tore you both apart
maybe this was when you hardened your heart?

We met after that *body*-ache
    brain-ache
        heart-ache
    soul-ache.
You were missing something from your life
    so you began your searching
        discovering…
            Me.

She was replaceable for a while
        with me by your side.
    Had everybody fooled
        I was the love of your life.
    But as is Fate
when *circles* round about
    you were destined in time
        for her to be found.

You tried to be casual
    acting coy and aloof
        but she looked so damned good.
    God
        she knew your *weakness*
through and through.

You thought
    just one taste of sweet
        blissful
    poisoned
        deviled lips.
She could never be as good
        as you set her up to be.
    But when you tasted her carnal lust
you became a *ravenous* beast.

The flames she set in you
          was desire
      set anew.
  And when the morning light arises
       you hang your heavy head
'cause you're ashamed
       of what you'd done.
  And she...
       she was gone from your bed
      again.

That was the very first time
       first time you *lied*
   to Me
with *fibs*
   or *diversions*
        or *revisions*
   of T R U T H.

And all it took was that one night
        she slipped right into
    our cozy life.
  It was
     as if
       she fit
     right in.

           I just never knew...

THE STONE COLLECTOR

I see the stones you bear
        upon your weary back
  as if you are a modern-day Sisyphus
reincarnated and condemned.

I ask to lend a hand
        seeking to lighten your load.
You reach into the netted bag
    cast across the expanse of your back
        and hand me a sizable stone.

Our fingers brush
  from this single exchange
and a spark pulsates
      through skin and cartilage.
You look at me
  with downtrodden eyes
      and say *you feel less alone.*

Asked once is nice
  but twice is more kind
this process on repeat
    as you continue to collect away
  always turning North
      my way
    in askance to lighten your load.

The day comes
  when weary head can no longer rise
and you cannot take another
     single step.
And as always
    I put out a pair of loving hands.

The boulder you pass off on me
    puts me in the ground
covers and consumes me
       leaves me suffocating
            without a sound.

I wish you would stop collecting.

But you are Sisyphus
   whom I cannot rescue.
These burdens are slated as yours to carry
    and hopefully
      you foster them soon.

'cause I…
   I am still buried in stone's weight
        from a desire to rescue you.
   And I am wishing on fake stars
 'cause the indigoed night is clear to me
     of everything
         but scars.

DISORIENTATION

Addiction hit me
    like a head on collision
  causing delusion and confusion.
      But
         I wasn't the driver.
             Maybe I'm not even a survivor...

I was more like an unwilling passenger
      in flight.
         I flew far from your sight
      begging for some Might
to save me.

I watched from the ground
      as my body hurled through the air
  in graceful synchrony
      from the impact.
     In-tact
    I landed as a disheveled sack.

I didn't ask to be on this ride.
All I wanted was to be by your side
    but never knowing
        the guide to your demise
  would rise to the size of grief
      with me
    attached to your side.

I felt I was "taken."
Taken and strapped in
      though I wasn't
  strapped in that is
     as this vehicle lost all control.

In a quandary over choices
        I never expected to make
  I hoped for my sake
      my soul it would not take.

        Still awaiting that verdict…

Forsaken in my daily life
        Addiction takes on a persona
          chasing me
with endless strife.

And in that moment
        when my lungs collapsed
   and I was concussed
I prayed to some god of Hope
      repeating to myself,
   "You are not alone.
          You are not alone.
      You are not alone."

THE SIEGE

We built a fortress
            gold glinted
     pure
  radiant
        stunning.
I thought it was rare
       this fortress we molded
    into our home
       malleable to our every wish.

We were the Architects.
     I the Artist.
          You the Builder.
  How could anything go wrong?
     You were my modern-day knight
        in plated gold
            though I didn't need one.

Or perhaps I was yours?

    I didn't need saving
   I was just a young girl
          looking for love.

We built a wall around our love
     solidifying our fortress.
         And when our energies were spent
   and the work was done
         we moved on
     forgetting the sweat and tears
     that went into building it.

This golden palace with caretaker on leave
    stood absolutely no chance
        when the weather heaved.

And as the gold melted amongst sweltering heat
    from Earth's tilted axis-
  gaping holes appeared
    and with them
      an open invitation
          to the enemy.

In one fell swoop
    all we dreamed up was breached.
      The destruction was so great
  I hid myself in the shadows of the gates
    watching in silence as you were captured
  by foes I once called "friends."

You did not come back to the keep that night.

I feared you were gone forever
      as I lay with your ghost.
  He was a melancholy comfort
      that I failed to breathe life into
    'cause I didn't realize
      I too had been captured.

LOVE IS BLIND

Can't share all the angry things on my mind.
Can't share all the words I forgot to find.
Can't share all the things I want to say
    so I leave them for another day.

I'm leaving them
    leaving them
  leaving them.

'cause
    I don't want to be that person
  the one that rants and raves
    the one that digs her own shallow grave.

'cause the pain and the angst
    I carry in my core
  is enough for involuntary tears
      to course in remorse.

They crop agile legs from where they start
    hacksawing and dumping them
      part
        by part.

So, I don't share my words
    though they are
      rip-screaming
    from my lips.
  I don't share my work
      gripping these worn-out hips.

All I do is sit here and think
    of all the things in my heart that sink.

Blink
        blink
    pushed to the brink
and I slowly let it settle in
      all the mistakes that I ignored.

Silently wishing for so much more.

And of the things I shouldn't have said?
   -I mull over the way they were expressed.
       And still I did nothing to move my steps
   to hasten myself down the darkened path
'cause to do so
      would have been to leave you behind.
     But I guess that's fine.
  'cause they say

        Love…

    Love

          is blind.

JUST IN CASE

Just in case you think lightning has struck
    I want to advise you that the storm is coming.
      That the storm is in fact a storm
    and not a warm summer rain
        where we bathe away our worries
  and dance the night away like gypsies
      …though we will dance.

I want you to know that my love will suffocate you
    because you are not prepared for it.
      And maybe it wasn't mine to give
    and yours to receive
        that we will blindly follow and lead
  because we think
    that *"that"* is what we are supposed to do.

That we will hit *"midlife crisis"*
    and not understand what it means
      as we hit it
        again and *again*
    on repeat.

And that I will tell you I hate you
    so that you will finally leave me
      because I *cannot* leave you
    because…
      I still love you.

And that we will become toxic chemicals
      that should not be mixed
    but we will be poured into one mold.
And our mixture will cause our lungs
      to heave from lack of oxygen

    and we asphyxiate
        over and over again
      while trying to live.

We will love each other
      as much as we will destroy one another.

And when you thought lightning struck that first time
      it was actually a warning
        that lightning will continue to strike
          until we become the ashes
            of falling
         debris.

Just in case you were wondering…

MILLIONAIRE

I could be a millionaire
    I swear it.
Like I have all my skin *and* yours
        in this game
            whether or not we wear it.
'cause *Fear* pushes itself out from each tiny pore
    burrows, digs, claws
        and then rips past the core.

If I could bottle fear…
    if I could sell *bottled tears*
        damn
    I'd be a millionaire.
I would *contro*l the masses
        with what not to do
    take love out of the equation
        as if I had a clue.

But boo-hoo, bleeding clues
    can't help me find
    what I'm looking for.
Some *cashless* shore
        with unyielding floors
            pouring liquid ashes behind
        ironclad doors.

And what is beyond the bank
    locked up?
        What lurks in shadows
    within *tinctured* cups?
Look into the mirror
    past that blurry haze.
        Deeper than your memories
    'til your shattered eyes are no longer glazed.

And when you blink from all you've betrayed
   remember all that I forgot
       'cause you have a tiny shot
   at dissolving the tangled knots.
But maybe not today.
   Today we posture and stay
       reminisce about the times and days
   our hearts were sitting on *layaway.*

'cause we ended the day
       scarred and scared.
      Within us it burns and sears
   our unindentured ears…
We become our *fear.*
       We become our *tears…*
and *still,* you refuse
     to kick recovery into gear.

And if I could bottle this-
   this-
     this fear.
Then my oh my
   I'd be broken-hearted
      but damn
       I'd be a millionaire.

SUBSTANCE

I wanted a life filled with the substance needed
        for love to thrive on.
   The love I found in you
       was the only *element* I believed in
           and I thrived in this environment.
        We thrived.

Ours was a love that knew no bounds.
       We exceeded the makeup of our bodies.
    This *matter* did not matter to us.
   We took on each test that crossed our paths
      and together were invincible
              until you pushed me aside
       and I became invisible.

The shift in our love was haphazard
         and our love lost all *substance*
     as you tripped and staggered.
And I never knew that your love
   could turn to inanimate objects
      and hold within it
the care and attention I was once afforded.

And now I understand
       why our marriage had no *substance*
  'cause there could be nothing present
       with the *dividing lines* of addiction
    separating us
   when your lust for it
      was resurrected.

WHOLE

I sit here and struggle with you pushing me away.
It is a great defense mechanism.
You are almost successful
    every
 single
       time.

I have no words.
There is a resounding silence every time I open my mouth
and even I cannot catch my words
   or
      my
                 b r e a t h …

I cannot hold onto words that do not exist.
And still I do not hate you.
I am just worried.

        Scared.

    Terrified.

           For You.

        For Us.

My heart is   CRA   CKED…
      Yours is too.
And maybe this is the only way we get to be together.
They did say two halves make a whole.
I just did not realize
        this is what "WHOLE" meant.

CABIN ON THE POND

The fog set in on this beautiful
    serene landscape.
Sprinkled in
       like salt and pepper
  to add a bit of flavor.

Beautiful and untouched
    pristine to the naked eye
  serenity oozing across the pond.

Melancholy in appearance
     the fog cloaks this cabin
      like an incantation of protection
        spelling away pain
     keeping it at bay.

I am shielded here
    holed away
       given opportunity
    to unburden my brain.

This beautiful scene becomes the foreshadowing
    …the calm before the storm.

And this is me
     trying to get back there.

HOPE CHEST

She packs up her *identity*.
   Neatly folded
      and into a beautiful case.
Each piece held
   and lovingly caressed
      clenched closely for a moment
  and then
    in it goes.

It is stacked until it is full.

She thinks she is done rebuilding
      foundations that
  crumble so.
Better to begin anew
   fresh blueprint
 commissioned
      at her request.

This case can be her "*hope chest*" dream
  heirloom of a promise.
    And maybe
  just maybe
she will revisit this
    beloved version
  of herself
      someday
    soon...

CRACK...

HOME

Muffled sobs amongst a party of tears
I was definitely invited here.
Playmates all sitting by my side
        Pillow
            Blanket
and *Sheet* don't hide.

They await shattered-composure's bones
      to turn to liquid and greet this home.
This space between contorted breaths
as I cry a hundred different deaths.

No judgment from this asylum I seek
just me and my *friends*
      as the dams start to leak.
So familiar is this pain.
        I'm here
    I'm *home*
           but I'm *insane*.

BLINDSIDED

I can't take it anymore.
I can't.
It's eating me from the inside out
like the acid I swallowed from your fucking lies.

On the outside
calm waters and beautiful views
like a forever
sunset horizon.

No one sees the churning currents
beneath the waters
as venomous words
course from your rotting lips.

You snort dreams like it's candy.
Met the Candy Man
and took a stand
just not the one I was expecting.

You stood tall for destruction-
wrecking balls were the theme.
And you dodged between them all
rejoicing in your victory.

You forgot to look back in your exuberance.
You missed the moment one took me down
and blindsided
I laid there stunned.

I was weakened in this state
confused over my love for you.
So I shot myself up with excuses
in an attempt to save you.

The wrecking balls
they kept slinging
one
by one.

Swishing
while I am here
wishing
to no avail.

The foundation of our home was rocked
cracked
razed to the ground.
And still nothing from you.

You were a corpsed man
in a living shell
and I…
I don't know what I was.

Maybe your corpse bride
with a side of hacked jaw
'cause I could say nothing at all
to move you.

WATERBOARDING

Your addiction waterboarded me
                    shocking my senses
             every time you *poured* your words
                over me.
    The *icy coldness* of it hit my lips
         my nose
      my skin
           the back of my throat
                  taking my breath away.

There you stood in the shadows
     a haunting silhouette
                 juxtaposed in our home
      dousing me in your shame
       'til I could no longer breathe
    controlling my every breath
                until I was no longer me.

And still
     you would not
   could not
        stop the *flow*.
You were finally "*in control*"
        of something in your life…

                M E.

Tied down by the weight of your lies
        I felt *helpless* to save myself
     though I *fought* with all my might.
  I watched from afar
       as a dissociated ghost

               Y O U

strapping my earthly body down.
    It was always *against my will*.
        And I can still smell your scent
      coming off your worn-out cloak
as you laid it over my face.

    It smothered me.

The scent I once loved
    became a symbol of my entrapment.

I lost a piece of myself
    each time-
      with every session.
  You drowned me
      on and off again
    endlessly.
  And all for a few minutes of *bliss*-
    of *heaven.*

What a price to pay
    for a false sense of joy
  for *peace...*

My heart was bartered
  bit by bit
  and now that you want it back
    there may be nothing of it
      left for you.

HOMICIDE

You apprehended me when you gave in to "giving up."
The steps I took to survive were no longer enough.
You were drowning in amber when you pulled me in.
Suicide turned homicide- Addiction for the "win."

I want to be gone and erased from your life.
I want your impact on me minimized.
A step or two taken to a wobbly tune
a cursed event revealed too soon.

The decisions I'm making are taking my breath
and not in a beautiful way.
More stolen and caged while my insides rage
and just as quickly I'm wiped away.

You shoot my heart with the bullets of your lies.
Keeping me down means keeping your disguise.
The air escapes from my heaving chest.
Left wondering…how one comes back from death?

REPLICATE

He walked away from you all when you were a child.
Your feelings of loss from his rejection began to pile.
The crushing blow of his departure was brushed away.
The issue was larger than you would ever say.

So much so you numbed your pain.
You stopped your growth for there was nothing to gain.
No more music played by strings
how crazy for history to replicate these things?

A loyal wife. Three kids- Girl, Boy, Girl.
You…leaving me for a life of cheap thrills.
Somewhere deep inside you hurt to this day.
Perhaps that's why it's hard for you to stay.

Here you are ready to leave
three beautiful pairs of eyes that grieve.
For the comfort of a man who they call, "Dad."
You leave them wanting…leave them sad.

Their eyes are mesmerizing just like yours
and they may recall this maddening discord.
I hope they will not replicate
the slow burning danger you perpetuate.

You are giving up on love…on me.
Though I've been by your side I'm the enemy.
There's no remorse for this course you paved.
You've chosen your path with no will…no willingness
    to stop and be brave.

CODEPENDENCY

Places, spaces, rhymes.
Places, spaces, rhymes.

Places where you are supposed to be
shadowed out by the pillars holding me up.
You are becoming a figment of my mind.

Places, spaces, rhymes.
Places, spaces, rhymes.

Spaces mapped out with room to squeeze you in
but you're too busy finding joy from the void within.
The space between us shifting into shadows.

Places, spaces, rhymes.
Places, spaces, rhymes.

Rhymes… *spinning…*
There are no rhymes- or reasons for these lesions
or this treason that spoon-feeds me   *m o n o t o n y…*

Places, spaces, rhymes.
Places, spaces, rhymes.

I am just looking for one wish to win.
One moment for love to shine.
For your eyes to open wide.

Places, spaces, rhymes.
Places, spaces, rhymes.

IT   DOES   NOT   STOP
this merry-go-round.
It does not stop…

Places, spaces, rhymes.
Places, spaces, rhymes.

There is just poetry to fill the gaps
words to help me mend.

And I still cannot find you in the places
the empty spaces
of my broken rhymes.

SAND CEREMONY

The heart vase, corked with white and blue sand, is sitting on display. I walk towards it and hold it in my hands. Its glass surface is as cold to the touch and as foreign to me as the memory of when we so lovingly mixed the sand during the ceremony of our marriage.

I walk to the table and pour the sand out. The sand runs over the glossy tabletop and glides along the smooth surface in a frenzy. I grab a couple bowls and a razor blade.

I want to make the vase match my broken heart, but I can't bring myself to do it. I'm sure I may regret my decision later, so I don't.

The beautiful sea of blue and white sand holds a beauty and purity that is blinding to me. Each one of these pieces, representing our vows. I sit down and I start sorting. White, white, white, white, blue, white, white. Blue, white, blue, white, blue, blue, blue.

The minutes pass, turning into an hour and then hours, as I start forming two tiny piles of sand. One white. One blue. I cup a bowl in my hands and quickly brush the tiny white pile into its hollowness. The sand whispers as it meets this foreign container. I do the same with the blue pile.

There.

The tiniest of dents in the sea of sand in front of me has been created. At least I now know that it is possible to separate our vows. Wondering if I can *un-mix* our hearts?

I think I can…

SNOW

Winter.
        Cold.
      Bleakness.
Pure
  white powder
sifting down
        down
      down.
      Blanketing the streets
            and *innocent lives…*

Winter dissipates.

        The

    POWDER

             does not.

The color of purity becomes
  all consuming.
      A dark force.

And I am choking
    on the remnants
  the
    trace
      memories.

THE OPPONENT

The trauma was so great by this time that I primed my heart for every step I thought you could make, playing against you like an opponent on the chessboard. I predicted your every move down to your "victories" 'til you thought I was defeated. And still I lay low with my every capture- unsteady with my every gain. Terrified of all I'd reveal with my very gaze.

Nothing was a victory.

I lured you into a gambit of carefully crafted resignation. Each pawn, a piece of me you were willing to take. And with each calculated step I take, the fury in me grows, but no longer like a that of a fire. I am out of time for learning to tame the flames seeking to consume me. My fury is more like the wind- erected by a perfect storm of devastation, and ready to wreak havoc on those trespassing my will.

Though I am closer to gaining the upper hand, I still don't know how to fight you. The path seems clear…yet I don't know if I am willing to take you down.

How do you destroy the person you love, to save him?

HOUSE OF CARDS

There's this house of cards that's been built.
                It's been stacked tall and wide
    with *secrets* built into each card
      each room
          and *locked* inside.

    I am *dismantling* this house
  one card at a time
and watch as you
        scramble to rebuild.

       G A M E O V E R .

No more games to play for this house of cards.

Just *steady hands*.
                Steady feet.
      Steady lungs that FILL with need.

    And when this B R E A T H is finally *released*
this whole house will fall into a scattered pile
          that I will *douse*
      with *gasoline*.

And when dancing *flame*
        meets
            sweet, suffocating, scent
    this deck will be naught
      but *ashes*.

    And if you want to *rebuild*
          you will have to find
      another
            deck.

THE BOMB

He wants to sleep and talk in the morning, and he doesn't even know that I can't sleep now. That with the ticking bomb he placed gently in my hands- I'm scrambling. I'm scanning my mind with an automated impulse to recall protocols that don't exist to dispose of this bomb...before it takes our house down...before *he* takes our house down. That with his words, or the lack of them, I'm wide awake. I'm mourning a man in front of me who is still present in form. And though he is here, he's concealed behind jagged lines of powder with the power to dismantle his throne...and mine.

Flashes of memories are flying past my eyes quicker than I can grasp them and all I can think is, "I can't lose my *Self*, my *Kids*, my *Life*." My feet want to move faster than I have ever been able to run in my racing mind, but they are frozen. In this moment, time comes to a standstill, and I can breathe again- though I can't catch my breath. This still-frame of the man I love, laying with his back turned to me...ticking bomb in my hands. Me, looking through the ceiling to where my innocent babies sleep.

There is one clear choice... L O V E. Love *does* conquer all. It just wasn't the love I dreamed of growing up. I gently place the bomb next to his static form. My heart blows him a silent kiss and leaves a prayer, heavy with hope. I slip away from the broken frame. Looking back at him, time has all but stopped.

Everything has changed.

EXTINCTION

On purpose
I pushed our relationship to the brink of extinction.
It was to save myself.
It was my last resort to save you…

It was only then
when the eruption of volcanic fires burned our forest down
that I could begin to see new growth
taking root again.

...SHATTER

THE GREAT ESCAPE

I need to get away from you. I need to not feel like your shadow is controlling me any longer, because you are no longer in control. *"It"* has you. The shade is cast so far and wide I feel I cannot escape *Addiction*. So, I stay. I stay and I devise a plan to leave you. It is $D\ E\ V\ A\ S\ T\ A\ T\ I\ N\ G$. I analyze all the traps you have set and disarm them one by one.

I am living with someone who is no longer my husband, no longer *You*. You push my hand daily to sell me *his* vision, where there is none. I am not buying your words, *his* words, anymore. And I am so sick of this *suffocation* keeping me on my knees as I continue to take my cues from you.

I take a step away from you each day, just like you taught me to- mirroring the moments of when you were sold on *abandoning* me. You taught me how to walk away with every word you spoke, every promise that you broke. You taught me with every step you took away from me and *all* the steps that never walked back.

This *apprentice* was mastering.

The day comes, and with it, a gnawing in my gut. Each conversation comes to a deafening crescendo where all my fears align. I had prepared for this very moment, and I am ready, though my heart is not. *I see my chance.* When your face and your words slice through me, it seals my resolve. And though I know that leaving you could mean you may be lost to me forever- I walk out the door and make my escape.

WHEN WRITE IS LEFT BEHIND

I cannot write today.
How can I write when writing feels wrong?
When right becomes left and left is left behind?
Everything is behind.
     Everything is behind and I'm supposed to forget
  because it's the past
        but the past has passed me by.

The future has to be now
          but now I don't know who I am.
I don't know who I "am" anymore
  because I am not "more"
        I am less…
     I am less happy.
        I am less loving.
   I am less trusting.
          I am less hopeful…

   …HOPE….

      …FULL…

I am full of air as hot as a balloon
   and I just wish my words would float away
  because I am raging inside.
     Raging from the blaze that you set forth within *Me*.

You set this blaze within and it is not a pretty thing.
And I cannot see with my own two eyes.
    Eyes that have been blinded by lies.
  And the lies
     they have compounded me.
     Compounded me into the ground pounded.

So now I just lie.
    I just lie low and I pray.
I pray and I pray
    and I say empty words
   to try and lead my broken heart astray.

    …astray from hate.

'cause, I hate, hate, hate my life.

Or rather
    I hate the life of "Us."
  Or rather
      I hate the life of "Love."

I hate everything that has come to pass
        for this agonizing chapter to end.

READY OR NOT

Courage comes for you
                whether you are *ready*
    or not.

I knew it from the   *r u n n i n g*

                        humming

      vibration of the floor.

My heart
    beating
  in anticipation of the crash.
        My body
    t h r u m m i n g with the echoes
                    of uncertainty.

And then silence.

          IMPACT

    …ready or not

                here it comes

        COURAGE.

        And I *j u m p* …

WOULD YOU KNOW IT?

Would you know this girl is desolate and in despair
        unsure if she could be repaired?
    When you see her smile
           and it lights up your life for a short while
              do you see she's holding on
      by less than a thread?

Thread that is U N R A V E L   L   I   N   G...

There's so much in her heart
        she's unwilling to shed
           'cause she doesn't want to burden you.
    She doesn't want to come unglued.

When she lends you her ears
      and gives you her undivided attention
    do you know it's because she senses
        you may need her?
   She needs you too
          to lessen her building tension.

Would you know it?

      I don't know if I would
   if I'm being honest.
        'cause I was her
           and no one knew it.

HOSTAGE

May my words S T A I N your memory.

        May they hold you H O S T A G E

    and L O N G I N G for peace

        the

      way

          I

              do…

BRAVE

She unleashes a forceful fury so unlike her gentle soul, and my stomach drops below freezing. It's negative degrees on this terrain of what is left of my soul. I know *why* she hurts and yet I cannot explain to her the emptiness and rage she is experiencing for the first time.

She is lost in her own wilderness with no forthcoming answer that "fits" into her image of the world. Her body convulses in swallowed cries of pain, and I tell her not to hold back the flood…but she does anyway. She *is* BRAVE, after all.

I feed her hope, like homemade cookies. Sweet and sugary and filled with love. And I listen to her almost incoherent words, "…but I don't know how to do that," she weeps. "…he held my hand and I fell anyway, and I just don't know how…" Her tears tell me she already thinks he is *lost* to her.

Glassy, doe-eyes, filled with despair at *"what-may-never-bes"* as if she is a fortune teller. All she sees are the tasks she could not complete- that she may never get to complete, because she is not sure he will be here. And it has to be completed with him…for there is no one else she calls, "Dad."

So, I hold her close and breathe her in, releasing love and breath into her, as if I can infuse her with my love. I let her cry and pray this pain will pass. I'm hoping these memories of them together will not be their last.

FATHER FIGURE

I worry for him.
I don't know if my love is enough.
I'm just his *Mommy* after all.
I question the future.
I question *everything*…

I watched his father grow up.
I saw his missteps.
He was always searching for something…
It's like I'm preparing for the replay
and I can't quite catch my breath.

He needs his Father
who I am not sure will be here.
And I am not enough
      though I love him
and the Man that helped create him.

He lays here in my lap
    quiet
        clingy
grasping arms that feel bereft.
I don't acknowledge his loss…

but I know he feels it.

BABY SOPRANO

She asks for him by name.
      Wants him.
    Needs him.
          I know this.

There are no words to explain his absence
            for ears
   so delicate
      so soft.

I show her images
        of his likeness
   instead
           and weep.

She is so grateful to me
  "thank you" repeated as her mantra
            in clear *baby soprano*
     and I shatter.

This is all I can provide her.
    Love.
        Pictures.
   Silence.
        Hope…

INNER TURMOIL

Countryside landscapes are out of my reach as I try to escape these winding roads. I am contemplating my breaking heart in a blur. My distorted vision is muddied water from watercolor brushes no longer used for creation. My eyes are forever wells of unfiltered rainwater. Tunnel vision is on the journey before me, and I don't know if I am strong enough to do this again.

Everything that has come before was concealed to me, blindsiding me in the aftermath of picking up the pieces. And maybe my thinking is wrong, but it was all about cause and effect…*cause and react*, for me. Someone once asked if I would have preferred to know my devastations in advance. I replied, "No."

Had I known the trauma I would come to endure, I would have chosen a different path. Had I known the impending impact, I don't know if I would have survived the betrayal, the lies, the abandonment, the grief. I would have "braced" for impact, and that may have made all the difference in the outcome of my journey. I don't know if love would have been enough. Most days it still doesn't feel enough, though I survived that trauma- albeit broken and bruised.

But now…now I have been blindsided again, and it's not about reacting to what has happened. The effects this time aren't going to end anytime soon. This time, it's about living *with* what is P R E S E N T in my daily life. All I see is the journey, full of pitfalls and loopholes. I'm not prepared for this climb, this *mountaintop goal*…this *being by his side.* I no longer know how to reach the top. I only know how to hold on, and I'm not as strong as I once was, though I am trying to be.

I'm terrified of the things I will have to face in the jungles I will traverse to reach the summit. How does one overcome that fear? For me it's not about overcoming, because that fear is here, living in me. How does one just put on boots, pack, and go? I'm sitting here, a mess of the person I once was, trying to lace boots that are too big for me. My bag is half-full of tousled belongings I'm not sure I even need. I'm unprepared to depart and still pondering why I must go.

DEAR GOD

If you do exist
    please stop the pain.
Mine hurts
  but
      please…
Please, please, please
   stop
     his.

LETTERS TO THE WIND

I'm writing letters to the Wind.
Each line written are words
      shredded from my heart
  that I can't get back
          which may be fine anyway.

I'm not so sure I've sent them correctly.

I write and then post it outside the window.
The Wind took it
  so
     that means something
  right?
         Or am I writing letters to myself?

I feel my words go unread.
  (Sender error?)
No response from the Wind.
    No matching letter returned.
        No shared shedding of heart.

My words won't stop this shedding.
They are falling to the ground
   even without my pen.
      Tired
     I scoop them in my hands
   walk steady steps
       towards chilled windowpane
    and release them out into the frozen night.

The Wind took them away.
     That means something
         r i g h t?

FROZEN RIVER

My pencil is blunt.
No matter how I try to get the words out
        nothing comes across these sheets.
Growth is happening like the cold freeze
        that has taken over this wasteland.
   Wasteland-
      my land.
     Always my land…

There's actually no land for me to stand on
        just tundra ice over running water.
    And I am frozen here
  praying that the sun doesn't come out to thaw this ice
and drop me into the churning currents.

The currents are running so fast now
        and all I can see are the possibilities.
    The possibilities of *F E A R*.
 I am immobilized
   with my fear of drowning.
     I can't swim
       and I'm standing on frozen water
     above a river of currents that seem to be circling me.
  I can't swim-
      and yet every step I take is towards the open water.

I no longer know how I endured these winter storms.
    I no longer know how I survived.
  All I know is this needling pain
   as my body starts to thaw-
      as I slowly become alive again.

It is excruciating
      this pain.

And *where* are you?

You know that I can't swim
        and you didn't come to save me.
           You're the one that dragged me out here
   and then you left.
          …you left me to drown.

I'LL LOVE YOU LIKE A SHADOW

I can't make you love me-
     can't make you see what you don't want to see.
  I can't make you love yourself or value life
       can't make you put down the carving knife
   that you use to make slivers of streaks on your heart
that you use to stab holes to bloodlet each part
           of the pieces of you that you despise
    behind a facade of angry
           red hues
     you try to disguise.
I'm walking away from the good and the bad-
    actually
      I am sad.
   'cause all I can see is the sea of
  "I can't"
        and nothing I do will ever change that.
  So I quietly love you
       like a shadow in the dark.
   And only you'll know
         if my love
     has hit
       its mark.

DISTASTEFUL SONG

The clickety-clack of keys rings in my ears
a distasteful song I want to un-hear.
It's the music of searching for help from a screen
as my fingers stumble and my insides scream.

The compression of keys the crescendo…then silence
becomes the deafening sound of violence.
You once again disappear into darkness
promising me your addiction is harmless.

If it were true, why does this tune play on?
Why am I searching this screen- creating this song?
My body knows what it is like to sway
your agitated moves are a dead giveaway.

I wish that I could make it stop
turn off my phone and let it drop
into a hole that never ends
instead…I just keep hitting *send*.

WHAT ARE YOU GOING TO DO?

What are you going to do?
    What are you going to do when there's *nothing* left?
        You act like this *well* will not *dry*.
    As if you can continue on
          F O R E V E R
      when the drought is nearing your side.

But what is *forever?*

You can only go *"forever"*
          'til forever is no more.
    You will only go "forever"
        'til you are two sheets
      feet first
          out the door.

What are you going to do
              when there is nothing left?
    When the hunger and thirst come to call?
    What are you going to do?

        What are you going to do?

What are you going to do when you cut off your limbs?
    Your branches can *feel* what you've done.
    What are you going to do to *protect* them?
And what are you going to do if they *break-* like you?

The high will *not last* forever.
    So, my love…
    when it all ends
          what are you going to do?

SHADES OF TRAUMA

I see you and I'm there again.
T H E R E...
It's this place in my mind
where I'm shackled to your lies
and your truths.

And I can do nothing but try to believe
the words coming out of your mouth
are the truth.
I always wonder if you believe
your own words...

'cause if *you* don't believe in the words that you speak
then how can you expect *me* to believe?
The *truth* is written across your face
you're unhappy
I'm healing at a snail's pace.

Yet how do I *H E A L*
when I have to face my *trauma*
Y O U
head on, each and every day?
How do I heal when I'm unable to verbalize my pain?

I know you are made up of all the colors in the world
but all you're giving off is blue.
And you could argue it's my *favorite* color
I just never knew that SHADES of blue would be
equivalent to *T R A U M A.*

LOOK

To paint your mind of the phrase
    "I am broken"
  and all that *that* entails
      may have you assume mistakenly
    that my heart is utterly frail.
And you would be right
  though also wrong
    I am as *weak* as I am *strong*.

And when I say that I am weak
  I mean
I am *the picture of pain*
I mean
    I am made of *small victories* gained.
  I reek heavily
    of contorted breaths
    lungs dialed down to agitated unrest.

This titanic love that we designed
    took *two* to help meet its demise.
 So when I say that I am strong
  I mean
    I know where it went wrong.
'cause I watched as you *destroyed* all we loved
  but little, broken, Me?
    I did *nothing* to try and stop you.

So…I know where I belong.
    I know this ugly song.
  'cause doing nothing was doing something
    just look at where we are.
      …look…

HOW DO WE REWIND TIME?

Your self-mutilated chemical dependency
brought your mind to new heights
where you stand alone
    though it is only in your mind.
  You actually can't stand.

You were always a brilliant mind
always beaming, always burning- like the sun
giving off a love so radiant
  it was a magnetic force pulling me in.

How do we rewind time?
How do we find a map
to get you back to your *Self*?
How do we get back to *Us?*
  And do you want to?

PICKING UP THE PIECES

FAULT LINE

I'm empathetic to a fault.
Like the line of San Andreas
it's biggest earthquake
        left the oceans dry
with only the salt from my tears
     remaining.

SILENCE

A deafening silence grows behind plugged ears.
You are in *recovery* and I am censoring my words.
Once again
I am silenced by you
        though inadvertently.

I am stuck inside skin that feels a size too small.
My heart is expanding at an uncontrollable rate
absorbing love, growth, encouragement, life…
It is everything I have hoped and prayed for
        and I *cannot…will not* contain it.

I am preparing for a life of fulfillment
refusing to *color within the lines* of love.
And you will not understand it right now.
So I remain silent
        biding my time 'til you truly heal.

CANDLES

I light a candle for you because I know you are lost. It's in the window of our bedroom. The candle moves with bated breaths as it flickers from solemn, but hopeful air.

I light a candle for you in my heart because you have lost love, though it is not mine you lost. My fingers are folded in crushed stalemate, as I whisper wishes into darkness that doesn't answer. And yet, I know your heart is still alive. I feel it. A piece of you still loves the man inside.

I light, I light, and I light. And I would light a thousand more if I knew it would shine out the darkness that swallows you. And I will continue to light until your unsteady feet find their way home, for this is your haven. Near or far- beyond the recesses of your mind, these candles are beckoning you like my heart's constant beats.

A rhythm just for you.

WANTING AND NEEDING

I want
      I want
    I want.

I want a hug so engulfing
      my sinking soul is caught
    netted in a grasp so tight
          there is no doubt hope exists.

I want bedroom conversations
     of a world we will conquer
with kisses nuzzled in.
      A safe haven
          found in nooked crevices
of neck and shoulders.

I want the feeling of time
      to stop
    allowing me to bask in intimacy
        we have crafted.

I want
      I want
    I want.

          I need...

I need to know your steps won't falter
     as we clumsily waltz through rugged terrain
   misstep after misstep
        but
           no sauntering away.

I need an honesty so bared
    we shatter
      before piecing ourselves together
        bit by bit
           but always together.

I need memories of you
    of us
      superglued in my mind.
The image- confirming a permanence
        to prove you were once mine
    ...*are mine.*

I want
    I want
   I want.

        And I need.

    Oh
      how I need.

THE LIGHTHOUSE (KUV TXIV)

He is a man of few words. He has never wanted for more than a simple life. He often praised me for what I accomplished, no matter big or small. He always responded with love and encouragement and never had to sell me on his love. I felt it every day and still do.

He is a gentle man. His promises are binding. He loves deeper than I have seen others deserve at times, but he doesn't care. He loves anyway, regardless of the price.

I am just like him.

His follow-through is concrete. I never worried when he told me not to. When my life fell apart and I had no words, he didn't promise me it would be okay. He told me, "Shh…my child. Don't cry… I don't know why this happened, but I am here for you." His words and the calm resolve in his demeanor gave me a renewed strength to move forward.

He called me often afterwards, to ensure I was okay. I wasn't, but I wasn't yet brave enough to tell him. I love him so much for his words. He was my lighthouse during my weakest moments, guiding the ship of my emotions to safety and infusing me with his light. His light was unwavering in its guidance to ensure I wasn't engulfed by the relentless waves of trauma.

The Lighthouse…Kuv Txiv (My Father).

THE WARRIOR (KUV NIAM)

I was embraced by arms that have held and lost too much in one lifetime. As I was engulfed by her warmth, I held my breath so she couldn't feel the pain within me reverberating to the surface. Her constant rhythmic heartbeat and her discerning eyes unearthing the bones of suffering I had buried.

She- tasked with keeping my soul topsoil-shielded. Her warrior spirit didn't need to hear the words in my heart to know I was in pain, though I was afraid to show her. I wanted to be strong, just like she taught me to be. I wanted to prove to her that I was built like she was. I should have known better. Showing vulnerability isn't weakness. It was okay to let out my breath and ask for help.

Her love knows my soul stronger than the cord that once connected us. I should know the power of a mother's love. I was too broken to see it in that moment, yet she knew it all. My heartbreak…heart-rupture. And she loved me anyway- for not being strong enough, for all my flaws, for all my white lies. That love…that power, is one of the most powerful forces in the world. She is my hero and words cannot describe how much I love her.

The Warrior…Kuv Niam (My Mother).

INSIDIOUS

The sun rises.
    A stark contrast to *festering* thoughts
growing darker in my head.

       H O P E...

    Hope is walking a tightrope
no safety net in sight.
The balancing act of wobbly teeth
      in a mouth of precarious words in flight.

  Betrayal is the white noise
      putting me to sleep.
But I don't wake up rested
  arrested instead
      in my own failings.

     Cold metal meets the exposed flesh
of back, arms, thighs, legs...
    I am *captured* now
full attention to the flaws inside my empty chest
victim to an ideal of love
    the *perpetrator*
      M E.

The universe oscillates
    weeping alongside my downpour.

    And still *I am lost*...

    Loving you is a jagged knife's removal.
Loving myself
    becomes the *gaping wound*
I am carefully repairing with band aids.

HOW DO I LOVE YOU?

I'm floating through days of silent misery
    consumed by rabid thoughts of,

"How do I love you…?"

And how do I handle your response
      to the perceived notions of my actions
    when I'm still searching for the answer?

You may not realize that the ending to that question is,

"…if I don't love myself?"

NOURISHMENT

How much can the heart break?
      Piece by piece it's shaved away
   'til there is nothing left
          and I am stuck here with the pain.

As our love continues to be forsaken
     and I leave you in the dust
          I drop the broken pieces on the trail
    as day old
       leftover crust.

How much can the heart break?
      Piece by piece until it is gone.
   I will move on
    though I feel empty inside
resolve is building through determined eyes.

I will light up the pages of our past
   burying the ashes as they float on back.
      They become the sacrificial nourishment
   repairing my broken heart.

COMPOSING

To understand the impact of the fall from the mountaintop, one first must know how great the journey was to get back up on two feet and onto solid ground.

…

You ask why I am broken. Why picking up the pieces of my heart is so hard. You ask why I keep looking back instead of forward. I do not think you understand- my feet are on solid ground for the first time in a long time and it wasn't my choice to climb down.

I was pushed.

I lost my grip on this climb called love, on this climb called life. I am still healing from the fall. It was not a graceful landing, and it took every fiber in me to force myself to stand again…to stand my ground. To fight for my life…to fight for love.

You misunderstand my hesitation…my pause for breath.

I am not looking back. My feet are still firmly planted. I am looking at the summit and I am mapping my ascent. You see? My feet are steady for the first time in a long time, though my heart is not steady. It is pounding in anxious rhythm, to a beat that has not yet been composed. And for the first time in our relationship, I am the composer.

…and I am composing the climb.

BEACONS

When I thought there was no fight left in me
    no air in the bags of my chest
        it was *You* who picked me up.
You who made me believe
        incoherent thoughts
        mattered.

You let me purge all the things I couldn't say
        to him…
    I was given time to digest the pain
        'til I could steady my breath.

And when moments became too dark
      and I felt abandoned
           You called me back from the blue
    like a beacon.

Poetry saved me
        I do believe…but so did *You*.
          Each one of *You*.
    You sent words
           prayers
                love
        and lent your ears.

And I cannot express enough gratitude
    for the way *You* picked me off the floor
        reminding me of who I am.
          Reminding me that I don't have to sacrifice myself
        for love.

You listened.
    And for that
        I am forever grateful.

A DECIPHERED PROMISE

Looking for answers on an empty page
        wide open space
    empty for ages now
            it seems.
Thirsty for the knowledge and truth
      hidden within
    hidden deep like the sea.
Secrets, always secrets
         within this hollow keep.

I'm unsure where to start
         how to navigate this pen.
   I place my shaky hand down
           with cold pen to bleak page
      and the ink starts to spill on its own.

What are these words
         that magically appear?
   Where does this writhing pain come from
      and how did I not know it was there?
So I search these lines
        re-reading each broken word
   and I find a deciphered promise
        much to my surprise.

This
    this was the silent promise
        the promise of a lined page
    inked page now-
filled with the whispers of my pen.
And through these scrawling words
       painful healing.
    But finally
        healing.

INSIDE YOUR SKIN

I wonder how it feels inside your skin.
    Does it sting you mercilessly like needles and pins?
    Do you wear it as comfortably as you wear your lies?
      Do you use it as a cover to cower and hide?

And if I knew how you felt in your skin
    would it have stopped my head from this dizzying spin?
    Would it make me stay in love with you?
    Would I believe your words to be any more true?

If I took a walk inside your skin
      would I be able to see past the endless abyss?
    Would I ignore all that went amiss?
 'cause I cannot see past the curtains of pain.
  I cannot see past the forthcoming shame.

And yet
   I sit here peeling away at each layer
     silently living on fractured prayers
   for if I could walk a day in your shoes
I'd probably come unglued like you.

Maybe…?

   Maybe not…?

How does it feel to be in your skin?

THE FOREST

The forest of our lives is nothing but our words
    planted as seeds
        and nourished by the sounding
repeated breaths used to create it.

These seeds took root in our lives
    and in our minds
        growing and growing and growing.
Your words and mine…growing.

This Forest does not belong to you
    does not belong to me.
        It is intermingled by the vines of our design
from the beginning of time, and we will never be set free.

We cannot deforest our forest
    without taking us both down.
We cannot burn the branches
    stopping us from tracking each other around.

But we can plant new seeds from different trees
    with root systems deeper than our peace.
        We planted once. We can plant again.
I'm hoping you'll come through.

Please… hold my hand with your gaze
    release a promise or two.
'cause I am hoping that it's true
    for love to be enough to see us through.

It was always this vision that kept me afloat
    a forever Love in this forest we grew.
It was a forever *Me*
        and it was a forever *You.*

THE HUNTER

I just want to see your eyes light up again.
   I just want to see you love yourself
      and your inner child.
         I feel like this is all I have dreamt of.
   It is all I have prayed for.

Shovel out all that dirt
   you have piled on your grave.
   Don't deprave yourself with the fabrications
      you groomed yourself to believe.

You are more than the meat in-between your flesh.
   I wish that you'd uncover it.
Please rip your skin from the lies haunting you.
   That trap you set was not meant for you.

You laid it out as your defense, and tense
 at the void within those teeth, you went looking for folly.
It must have hurt when the shock wore off
    and your skin and broken bones were trapped
      in the teeth of your lies.

I see it.
    I recognize that pain for all its brokenness.
  What's broken must be reset
     one painful touch at a time.
And all we can do is wait for time to heal this pain
   …for time to heal Us.

So before you love me, please break your heart
   and I will hold your hand.
I will be your balm.
  and together, we can piece your heart bit by bit
     until you're strong again.

LITTLE BOY

Little Boy with questions in your chest, what are you reaching for? Are you searching for an unconditional glove to encompass your hand, refusing to depart? Are you yearning for acceptance, for the boy you were and the man you've become?

Faded memories of a shadow man who was here briefly, though his impact has echoed for longer than his presence. Footprints walking away from you, though you know not why. People leaving…always leaving. No one ever stays.

So, you stay, collecting the strays and feeding their souls. Most feed off you while leaving you flakes of their love. You, forgiving boy, heart and soul played like a toy with joy that must seem so far away. When someone stays, you are blind to the rays cast over your frozen form.

She wants the forlorn to be brushed from your eyes like the snow, the clearing, forming pathways to her hearth. Warm yourself in her ambiance. Revel in the heat forming deep in the pit of the stomach you forgot exists. See the burning flame that is lit for you there. Don't be shy- don't even try to deny the love that is yours to claim. Bask in the warmth of home, her heart. Its doors will always be open for you.

And Little Boy, those frozen footsteps will melt away with Spring's warmth, though this memory may remain embedded somewhere within. The years will fade this memory, though the imprint is woven into gut-and-feel. And when you jerk in pain from feeling, just know it's because you love so deeply. It's okay to hurt for those we love. It's okay to hurt. Just don't lose yourself from it.

FLUIDITY

Wondering if we can get back to fluidity?
    Where your touch and your caress
        glide over my skin
      like the gentle flow of water.

We were there.
    "There" where we would hold our breaths
        abated
            eyes ungated
   bodies undulated
                under blue hued skies.

We were lost.
        Lost in love
     in lust
          in moments held frozen
where no one existed but two warm bodies
    trying to rule the world
           and *not* each other.

We were fluid once upon a time
    You and I.
        Wondering…
            can we get back there?

MEAT IN THE MIDDLE

It's always on my mind… How to get back to "Us?" I don't have the answer. The people we were are forever gone, with only the traces within our eyes remaining. I hope to recognize the man I fell in love with. I would love to feel his warmth again.

I know it won't be easy. I know that they say a person's choice is out of your hands, but that doesn't mean I had to let you go…that I had to give up on you. I don't regret fighting for you or your life- for the kids, for me. I don't regret fighting for love.

There is just the issue of this meat in the middle of our chests…what do we do with that? How do we heal? How do we protect a new love? How do we fortify it?

Meet me in the middle as we set forth on a new journey. I will pray we have garnered wisdom so that history does not repeat itself. I will pray for trust and patience and communication.

And I will always stand by your side, even if we aren't meant to be. You are after all, my greatest love.

THE MASK

I sit here, a picture of *serenity* painted on my face.
        An accustomed image
      I've come to *mask* my true self behind.
It becomes easier to paint the *facade*
           as expected responses are *easier* to navigate
than what is truly found
          beneath the surface…

    or so I thought…

The *reality* is
         my scars are screaming loudly in *calamity*
    burning *truth* through the scars
         and reopening them.
      The wounds
           healing
     were merely bandaged
to stop the flow of *pain* and nothing more.

Unearthed now, these *scars*
       with their jagged ridges
throb for attention.
         This time, I take *care* with my flesh.
      I gently soothe the pain with *whispers of love*
           hoping my skin absorbs the *wishes*
    renewing my resolve.

I watch and bide my time as
       regeneration
           restores
      healing.
And this mask that was becoming so familiar
           is now *unbearable.*

I ache to be seen for who I am
    for who I was always meant to be.
                  This
          is
                  M E
                                learning to be whole
        as I unmask the stranger
                who had taken over.
She is gone now
        banished by a stronger warrior
      a hidden *Phoenix*.

              P L E A S E…

                    rise with me.

RESCUED WISHES

I went back another day
        just like I said I would.
    It felt like the right thing to do
            and the *change* was waiting for me.

      …I was waiting.

I was waiting for breath.
          Waiting for it to move
    in and out
        of lungs
          deprived of relief
              for too long.

The stones of the wishing well are still chilled
        as is the change.
    They seem even more forlorn
           since I left them that day.

   But no more.

        Not after today.

     You see?
        I brought another piggy.

I kneel by the wishing well-
      He an old soul by this time.
   He saw all the wishes that went in
         all the dreams that didn't come true.

But I came prepared today
              to rescue each one of you.

Piggy sits like a champion by my determined side
       catching each weathered coin
           clinking musically
   as they are dropped in
               one
      at
             a time.

And with each jingle
            resounding from her filling belly
     a melodious sound protrudes from my lips.
      … for we were finally

RESCUING

WISHES.

WORTHY

I am worthy.
                I am worthy.
       I am worthy.

These are the words I never said to myself.
     These are the words I placed upon the dusty shelf.

When life hit me to the ground
                left me shuddering with a frown
      my grin became akin to uncertainty.
             Discord- my enemy for eternity.

I lost it all…

This crown no longer on my head
      it doesn't shine, it's bleeding dread.
     And the answers don't come coursing through
        they are stagnant 'cause I never grew.

No more.
            No more.
       No more.

I can no longer take this hurt inside
    can no longer stay on this bumpy ride.
  I'm taking a stand to end my pain.
    I am worthy.
       I have so much to gain.

I am worthy.
               I am worthy.
      I am worthy.

And I'm going to *pave* my own way.

Acknowledgements

To my family: I would not be where I am today without your unwavering support. You stood by me and sometimes carried me. I could not have survived addiction and written this book without each of you. I am forever grateful for your roles in my journey towards healing and publishing.

To my friends: You know who you are. The ones who helped to pick up the pieces of me until I felt myself again. You listened, without judgement and let me just *be*. Your words of love and kindness were priceless. Thank you.

To my Instagram community/friends: Your words and honesty allowed me to push the boundaries within myself as a writer. I draw from so many of you artistically. Your prompts and words have pulled inspiration out of me, allowing me to express my journey in ways I never expected. Thank you for being you and for showing up.

JUST IN CASE is inspired and written after, *Fair Warning,* by @dempoems, on Instagram.

A DECIPHERED PROMISE is written using the prompt, "promise of a lined page," from her book, "Poetic Self-Portrait," by @caroline_creativecorner, on Instagram.

THE MASK is inspired by the prompt lines, "her scars are screaming loudly" and "learning how to be whole," from poetry written by, @storm_writing, on Instagram.

About the Author

S.Z. is a Hmong American writer from Wisconsin. Her works are composed from her life experiences. She also pens under E.Z. Putnam (@esszputnam) on Instagram and Facebook.

"I have hidden myself for far too long from fear of being different due to cultural and self-imposed restraints. I have decided to let go of all expectations and personally grow through emotional healing and move others to do the same. No one person should have to manage trauma on their own."

S.Z. has had a love affair of writing her entire life and was always consuming works of literature in her youth. She continued writing in college and thrived while expressing herself through her words. After trauma in her personal life, she stopped writing and only recently resumed; this time with poetry. She has found poetry as an insight to her mind in helping her navigate her healing journey.

Her poem, "The Storm" appeared in the magazine, *The Auctores Monthly: July 28, 2021* (The Auctores).

This is her debut collection of poetry and prose.

www.SZPutnamPens.com

Reviews

"S.Z welcomes the reader on a rollercoaster journey with hands clenched on the bar rail of vulnerability and granular introspection. In this collection she highlights the true meaning behind unconditional love and perseverance while navigating trauma. This book is a manual for healing and a catalyst for change. She is a true advocate, headlining that broken doesn't have to stay broken."

Ramon Carty, Poet @ramrock_speaks on Instagram

"In Loose Change: Picking Up the Pieces, S.Z. Putnam is the architect of her story, told artfully through poetry and prose. So many pieces create vivid scenes and emotions on their own, but read together, these works capture the highs and lows of her journey in a way that will no doubt tap into the reader's own visceral experiences with heartbreak and recompense."

Pamela Smith, Poet @poetstale on Instagram

"S.Z. has lent you her voice and a peek into her life in a poetic style. She writes of how addiction has affected her life as well as her family. She shows strength in her ability to overcome the loss of her husband with so many broken promises given. How her parents held strong and stood by her side as this disease tore apart her marriage and family. This is poetry I highly suggest if you would like a look into a life affected by addiction and how to move forward and become a stronger mother and wife.

Written with a rawness that will break your heart yet open your eyes to survival. Sharing her experience takes great strength and I know this book will give hope to others who are still suffering. I am very familiar with addiction and this book has touched my heart and soul."

Rebecca Albaugh, Volunteer of 20+ years in addiction as well as a mother, grandmother and a partner with 30 years clean.

"In her debut collection, S.Z. Putnam takes us on a wonderful and encompassing journey, beginning with the first jolts of an electric love, followed by the appearance of fault lines in a crumbling relationship; then moving through loss and hardship, and eventually towards healing. Through her words, we are given a picture of loving through addiction and betrayal and the turmoil of being in love while knowing that sometimes love alone is not enough. All of this is presented with an honesty that cuts right through the page, and she shows us that though the fall to the bottom always hurts, the place where we belong is right back up the mountain, savoring the views along the way."

Robert Riichi, Co-Author of "No Man's Land: An anthology of men's poetry"

"Take a deep breath and prepare to read through a veil of tears, personable pieces of poetry and prose, where the only winners are the readers. A self-therapeutic telling of loving someone with an addiction."

Psalm, Writer @angela_psalm on Instagram

"With 'Loose Change: Picking up the Pieces' we are privileged to hear and witness the journey of one poet's discovery of self-healing, and ultimately of hope. S.Z invites us into a turbulent quagmire that in the hands of a lesser writer could become too much to bear, but she has skillfully used form and imagery to lead us into the darkness and back out the other side. This collection is, at heart, a love story, but also far more than that. The all encompassing infatuation that comes across in 'Nothing' becomes the heartbreak of 'Tattooed', until the bleak realization of 'I Lost You' settles in. This could have been the tragic demise of a relationship that ends there, but instead S.Z has allowed us a glimpse into the messy world of addiction and the hard work that recovery involves. 'The Stone Collector' is an especially poignant nod to the uphill battle that an addict has to fight for themselves, while the last two chapters 'Shatter' and 'Picking Up the Pieces' give us particular insights into her own resilience.

It was an honor to read these words in the pre-publishing stage, and even more of an honor to count her a friend."

Charlie Thomas, Poet @storm_writing on Instagram

"A raw, visceral and deeply immersive exploration of the impact of addiction on a relationship and a family. Love, betrayal and desperation are delicately counterpoised with hope and the potential for redemption & renewal. A profoundly moving & insightful debut.

Tash Haigh, Poet @truth.seahorse on Instagram

"S.Z's words colorfully display the woeful battle that comes with the damage that addiction can bring, but also how the pain can be harnessed and used as clay to mold her poetic journey. The book opens by setting the stage with the way things were and takes you through the levels of discovery, disappointment, internal struggle, and inner strength, brought on by her partner's battle with substance abuse.

A myriad of brilliant metaphors, similes and rhyme schemes beautifully outlines her strength and vulnerability amidst the tumultuous times she endeavors to learn from.

From the aptly titled "First Time" to the triumphant piece "Worthy," you will be on the edge of your seat and reaching for the tissues. Her well-crafted word play will have you aching to read more, and in awe of her masterful use of language.

Kheneil A. Black, Writer @kheneilblack on Instagram